FROM FINS TO HANDS

An Adventure in Evolution

ALSO BY ANTHONY RAVIELLI

Wonders of the Human Body
An Adventure in Geometry
The World Is Round

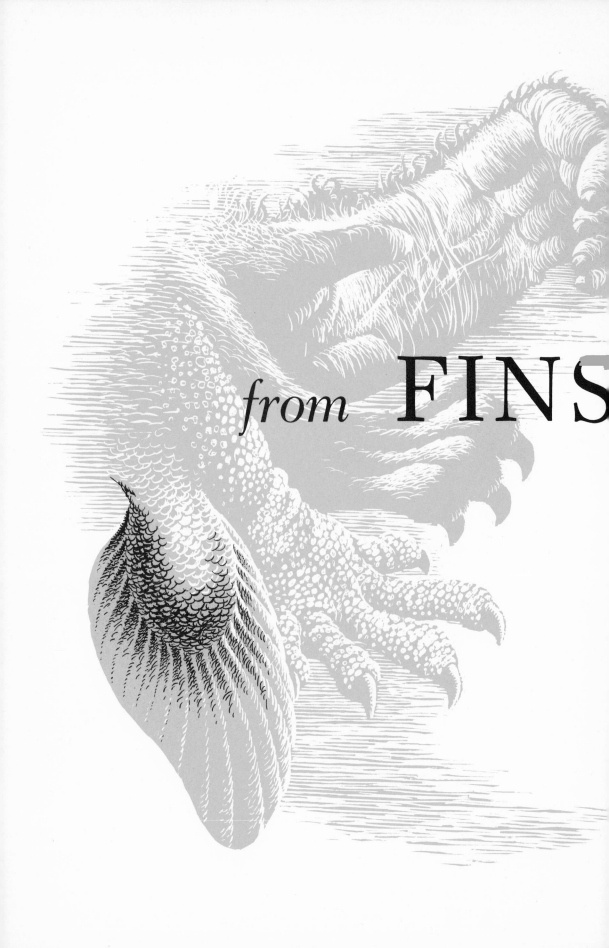

from FINS

TO HANDS

An Adventure in Evolution

WRITTEN & ILLUSTRATED BY

ANTHONY RAVIELLI

THE VIKING PRESS   NEW YORK

First published in 1968 by The Viking Press, Inc.
625 Madison Avenue, New York, N.Y. 10022
Published simultaneously in Canada by
The Macmillan Company of Canada Limited
Library of Congress catalog card number: 68-27574
Printed in U.S.A. by Halliday Lithograph Corporation

573   1. Evolution of the hand

To Zoopy — a happy handful

Suppose we had hoofs or paws instead of hands. Can you imagine how different our lives would be?

A horse or cat, even if it had a human brain, would not be able to perform such commonplace tasks as lacing a shoe, buttoning a shirt, turning a knob, or holding a toothbrush.

We are superior to the lower animals not only because we can think, and can communicate our ideas, but also because we possess hands capable of carrying out the wishes of our remarkable brain.

Our hands enable us to make and use tools, to play musical instruments, to draw, to write, or to turn the pages of a book when we read. They can pluck a fragile flower without crushing it or smash a walnut with a single blow.

Almost every human activity calls for the use of our hands. Even when we talk, we often rely on gestures of the hands to make our words more meaningful.

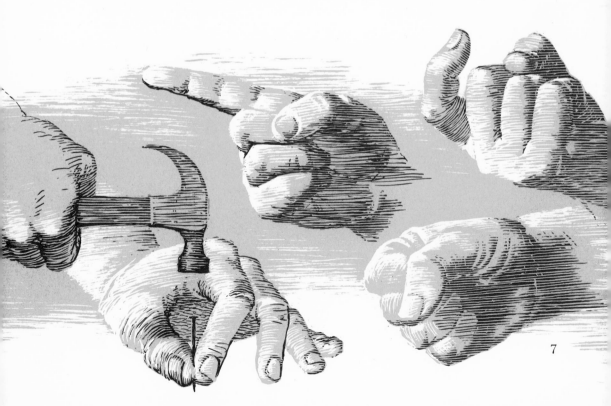

The basic structure of hands, like that of other bodily features, is not unique in human beings. It was passed down to us through a long line of ancestors whose limbs and bodies underwent drastic changes as they adapted to the surroundings in which they lived.

Each new group that appeared on earth had gradually developed those particular structures which gave them some advantage in the effort to reach food or to escape danger. Hands, feet, hoofs, paws, wings, and flippers are different structural forms that animals acquired through evolution in their struggle for survival.

Some of these structures serve but one function: to carry the weight of their owner efficiently in a specific environment. Hoofs, for example, are excellent tools for running swiftly over the flat ground. Wings are for flying only. And a seal's flippers, which were once limbs, have become so highly specialized for swimming that they are cumbersome out of water.

Fortunately for us, at about the same time that some animal limbs were being molded into such specialized forms, the evolution of human hands and feet took a different path — even though they had the same beginnings as the other animal appendages.

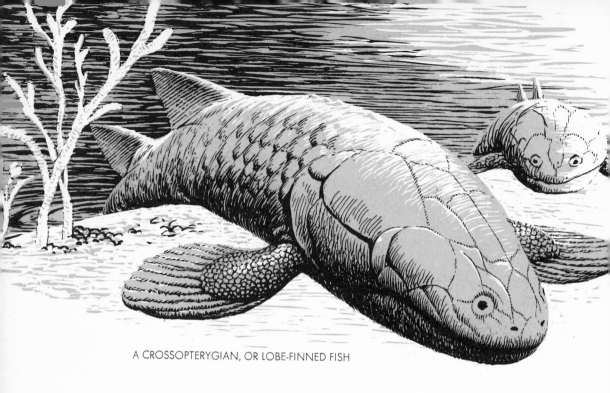

A CROSSOPTERYGIAN, OR LOBE-FINNED FISH

The first steps in the long march that eventually led to hands were taken by a group of bony, lobe-finned fishes more than 300 million years ago. These primitive creatures were the first vertebrates — animals with backbones — to venture out of shallow waters and drag themselves along on dry land.

Although they had evolved in water, lobe-finned fishes somehow acquired the equipment to attempt that dramatic journey onto the land. In addition to gills, which they needed to breathe in water, they had an air sac that enabled them to breathe out of water as well. And their fins had developed into bulky, muscular paddles, strong enough to move the body over the ground against the pull of gravity.

The lobe fin looked like a round, fleshy stump with a fringe at its edge. Inside, it was braced with thick, bony supports that increased in number near the fringe.

Though originally designed for swimming, lobe fins made the invasion of the land possible and paved the way for new forms of life to develop on the surface of the earth.

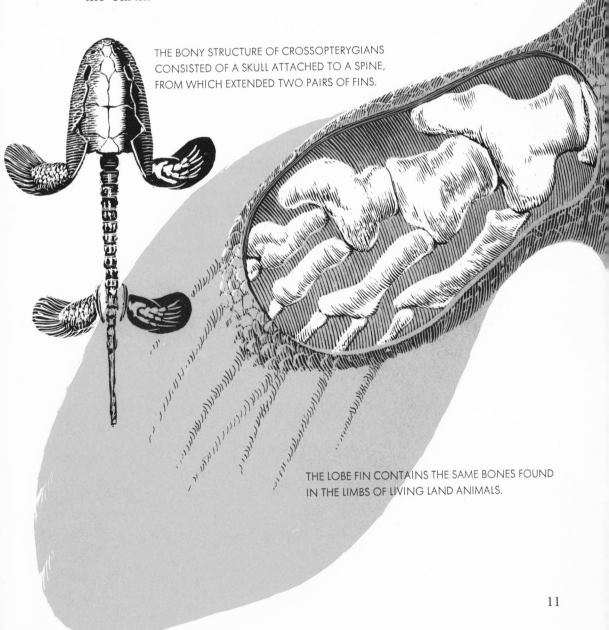

THE BONY STRUCTURE OF CROSSOPTERYGIANS CONSISTED OF A SKULL ATTACHED TO A SPINE, FROM WHICH EXTENDED TWO PAIRS OF FINS.

THE LOBE FIN CONTAINS THE SAME BONES FOUND IN THE LIMBS OF LIVING LAND ANIMALS.

11

In time, the lobe-finned fishes gradually evolved into amphibians, which, though born in the water, spent most of their adult lives on the land.

The earliest known amphibians resembled their lobe-finned ancestors. They even had a fishlike tail. Their fins, however, had become limbs, and the bony braces once hidden in the fringes of lobe fins were now extended to form a crude appendage.

The appendages of some primitive amphibians had five fingers, and others had as many as seven. But most had four fingers, as do the limbs of modern amphibians — the frogs, the newts, the salamanders, and the toads.

Though better for ground travel than lobe fins, amphibian limbs still flared out from the body like fins. At this early stage, vertebrate limbs did not support the body but dragged it.

ICHTHYOSTEGA, AN EARLY AMPHIBIAN

ERYOPS, AN ADVANCED TYPE
OF PRIMITIVE AMPHIBIAN

THE SKELETON OF ERYOPS SHOWS
WELL-DEVELOPED FRONT AND HIND FEET.

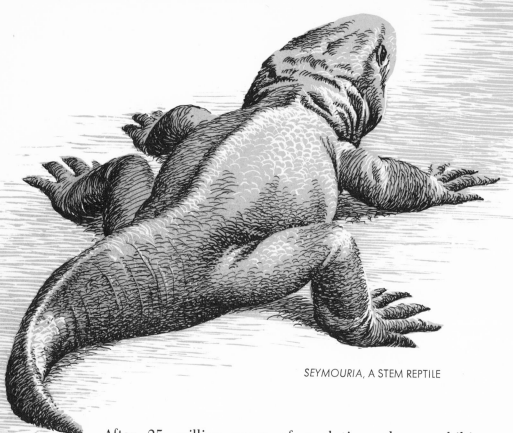

SEYMOURIA, A STEM REPTILE

After 25 million years of evolution, the amphibians no longer looked like fishes. But they were still chained to the shores of lakes and streams, because their eggs could hatch only in water.

Then, a branch of the amphibian family appeared which laid hard-shelled eggs that could hatch on land. From such eggs came the earliest reptiles — the first true land-dwelling vertebrates. Reptiles emerge from the egg fully equipped to spend their entire lives on dry land.

Although this astounding feat was a turning point in the history of life on earth, it had little or no effect on the physical structure of the first reptiles. They were built exactly like the later amphibians and moved as clumsily over the land as their water-bound cousins, because their short, stubby limbs still sprawled sideways from the body like fins.

With the belly hugging the ground, locomotion for the original, or stem, reptiles must have been difficult and tiring. But this new way of life was bound to bring about changes, and in time, it did — in the limbs of their descendants.

THE NUMBER OF JOINTS IN THE FINGERS AND TOES OF SEYMOURIA WAS TYPICAL OF THE EARLY REPTILES.

With the entire face of the earth on which to expand, reptiles evolved swiftly. Primitive reptiles were soon replaced by more advanced forms — some with strange sail-like formations on their backs.

Despite their peculiar appearance, these odd creatures were better adapted for land living than the stem reptiles. The most important improvement was in their method of moving about. Their bodies were carried on longer, more slender limbs with clearly defined elbows and knees. Walking was further helped by flexible wrists and broad appendages with fingers and toes of nearly equal length, so that they could push more evenly against the ground.

At that time these ancient reptiles were the dominant land animals. They were the first vertebrates to stand on supports modified exclusively for land use. And though their limbs still sprawled outward from the body, they could move rather briskly over the ground.

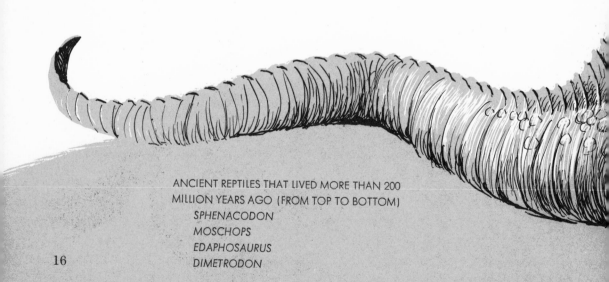

ANCIENT REPTILES THAT LIVED MORE THAN 200
MILLION YEARS AGO (FROM TOP TO BOTTOM)
SPHENACODON
MOSCHOPS
EDAPHOSAURUS
DIMETRODON

CYNOGNATHUS, A MAMMAL-LIKE REPTILE

The ancient reptiles gave rise to a wide variety of groups. Some evolved into the turtles and the crocodiles, and others into the biggest and most fearsome land animals that ever lived — the dinosaurs. But one group remained small and plain-looking. Their evolution took place inside the body.

We don't know how it happened, but these cold-blooded reptiles acquired many of the features found only in warm-blooded mammals. Their skull, teeth, backbone, and limbs were different from those of most reptiles.

Scientists refer to them as mammal-like reptiles — the forerunners of mammals, the warm-blooded vertebrates that bear their young alive and nurse them through infancy.

Mammal-like reptiles shook off completely the sprawling position that handicapped their more primitive ancestors. Their limbs were closer to the body for better support. This position not only raised the body high off the ground but also brought the elbows back and the knees forward, making it easier for the limbs to work smoothly.

Another significant improvement was the five-fingered paw with two joints in one of the fingers and three joints in each of the other four.

This arrangement of finger joints — exactly like ours — was passed on by the mammal-like reptiles to their mammal descendants about 200 million years ago.

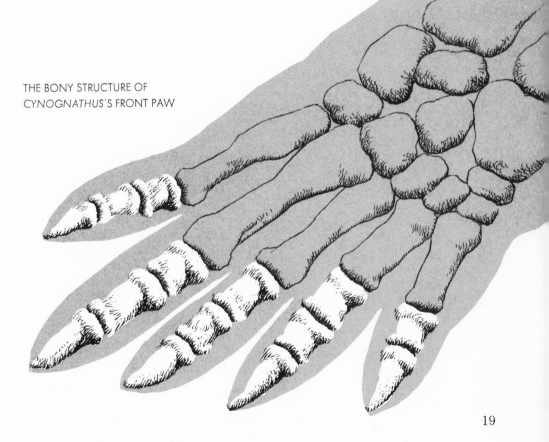

THE BONY STRUCTURE OF
CYNOGNATHUS'S FRONT PAW

The first true mammals appeared on earth before dinosaurs came into existence. They were small, mouselike creatures. So it isn't surprising that they remained inconspicuous throughout the Age of Great Reptiles.

Too small to compete with the ruling reptiles, mammals survived by staying out of the way of their gigantic and terrifying neighbors. They scurried in the undergrowth, bushes, and trees for food and concealment.

Despite their tiny size, mammals were superior to reptiles in many ways. They were smarter, more active, and far swifter. And, having warm blood, mammals were able to survive in any climate. With the sharp-clawed, five-fingered appendages inherited from their reptile ancestors, they could pin down insects, scratch for worms, dig holes in the ground for shelter, and scramble up trees for safety.

In mammals, appendages became flexible paws. Finger joints grew longer and the two-jointed finger moved to one side, suggesting a thumb.

Mammal limbs were tucked directly underneath the body. Their fore and hind limbs moved freely and rapidly — an important feature for climbing trees, chasing prey, or outracing the enemy.

About 70 million years ago, when the Age of Reptiles came to a sudden and mysterious end, the shy, timid mammals moved out into the open for their own evolutionary climb.

At first, their progress was hardly noticeable. Then, with a spurt, an abundance of vigorous branches sprouted from their flourishing family tree.

As the Age of Mammals dawned, the land teemed with a fantastic variety of new life forms. Mammals of every description emerged and overran the surface of the earth. Most of them bore no resemblance to their mouselike ancestors. Larger than their forebears, these new species of mammals underwent constant physical change as they adapted to the environment in which they lived.

In some mammals, the primitive five-fingered paw remained unchanged. In others, it showed signs of subtle refinements. But in the majority of mammals that populated the expansive plains, the limbs, hands, and finger joints were becoming drastically modified for highly specialized use.

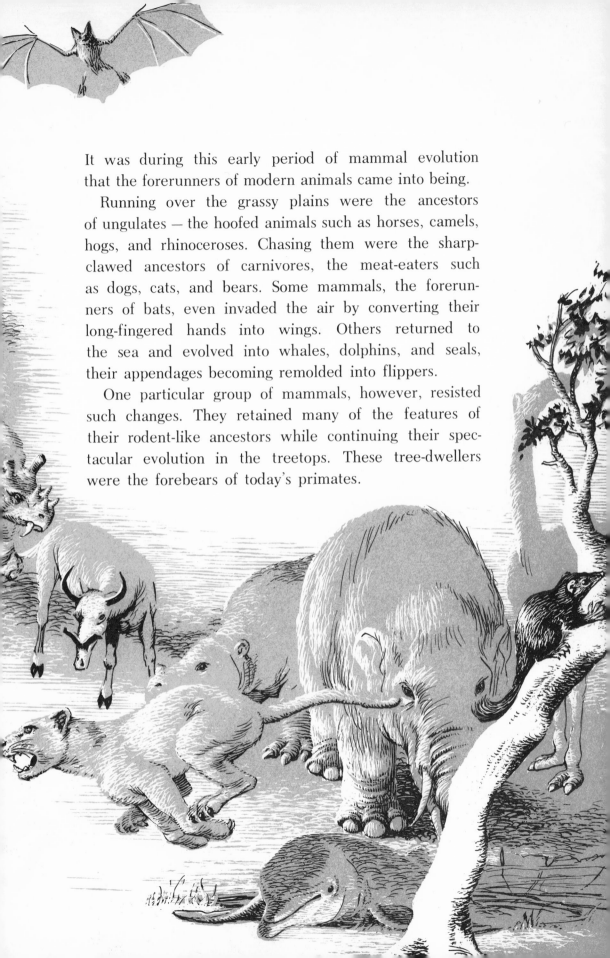

It was during this early period of mammal evolution that the forerunners of modern animals came into being.

Running over the grassy plains were the ancestors of ungulates — the hoofed animals such as horses, camels, hogs, and rhinoceroses. Chasing them were the sharp-clawed ancestors of carnivores, the meat-eaters such as dogs, cats, and bears. Some mammals, the forerunners of bats, even invaded the air by converting their long-fingered hands into wings. Others returned to the sea and evolved into whales, dolphins, and seals, their appendages becoming remolded into flippers.

One particular group of mammals, however, resisted such changes. They retained many of the features of their rodent-like ancestors while continuing their spectacular evolution in the treetops. These tree-dwellers were the forebears of today's primates.

The earliest primates closely resembled the modern tree shrew. Even at the beginning of their long career, these descendants of tree-dwelling mammals were well adapted to deal with their environment.

Of primary importance was the development of flexible hands with movable fingers, suited for climbing among lofty branches. Life in the treetops also made primate limbs somewhat different from the limbs of animals that walked or ran on the flat surface of the ground. The limbs of horses, for example, are restricted to motion along a single plane. Primates, however, could move their forelimbs with great freedom in almost any direction. Their hind limbs also moved freely but were becoming thicker and more muscular, to help support the weight of the body when climbing.

The early primate had still not shaken off the mouse-like appearance of its ancestors. It was a small creature with a long, pointed face and eyes at the sides of its head.

In the course of their evolution primates produced four main groups of tree-dwellers: prosimians, New World monkeys, Old World monkeys, and apes.

The prosimians, or lower primates, were the first to appear. This group included the ancestors of today's tree shrews, lemurs, and tarsiers.

Lemurs were not unlike the earliest primates. They too were small and bushy-tailed, but their hands were becoming more suited to arboreal living. Their thumbs, for example, were more widely separated from the other fingers — an advantage for gripping branches.

Tarsiers were a step higher on the ladder of primate evolution. A link between lemurs and monkeys, the primitive tarsier had extremely wide eyes, a flat face, very long hind legs, and an equally long tail. These saucer-eyed creatures were jumpers and traveled by leaping from branch to branch.

In the tarsiers, the hand underwent further modification. Its long, wiry fingers were tipped with disks to secure its hold on branches after leaping.

The first monkeys appeared on earth after 20 million years of primate evolution.

Considerably larger than the prosimians, monkeys were even better endowed for life in the trees. A notable advance was the well-developed hand with a rotating thumb, longer, more flexible fingers, and flat nails, instead of claws or disks, to protect the fragile fingertips.

These improvements converted the hand from just a climbing and clinging aid into an efficient grasping instrument. With a thumb that could come around to help the other fingers grip a branch or pick up a tiny insect, the hand of primitive monkeys not only made locomotion in the trees safer — it made the seizing of food and other objects easier.

In addition to grasping hands, the primates also acquired binocular vision. Binocular vision means that both eyes are on the same plane at the front of the head and can focus together on the same object. With binocular vision, distance can be judged accurately and objects can be seen more clearly in relation to their background.

Being able to see what was directly in front of them, monkeys could react quickly to any event that occurred in their treetop world. With both eyes working together, they could identify food more easily and observe things more intently.

The placement of the eyes at the front of the head had an even more significant effect: it changed the structure of the primate skull, increasing the area of the skull cavity, and allowing a different type of brain to develop — a brain in which the visual center was greatly enlarged.

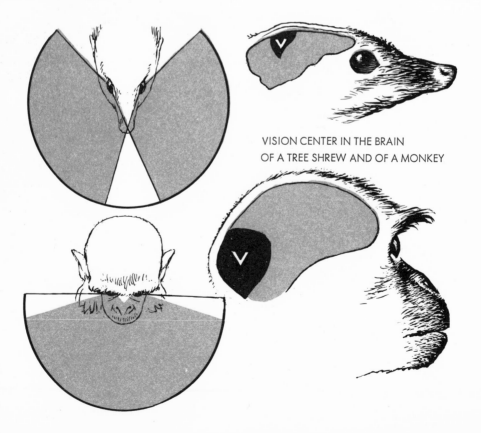

VISION CENTER IN THE BRAIN
OF A TREE SHREW AND OF A MONKEY

With a larger brain to direct movement, monkeys used their eyes and hands to greater advantage. Each new group that evolved was more efficient in climbing and better at selecting safe branches on which to walk. Eventually monkeys learned to reach out, grab, hold, and examine whatever grew or crawled in their jungle habitat.

In a relatively short time, monkeys became the cleverest and most expert of the tree-dwellers.

As monkeys reached the peak of their evolution — about 25 million years ago — another branch of the primate family made its appearance. These new primates were the forerunners of the anthropoid apes — the gibbons, orangutans, chimpanzees, and gorillas.

Though related to the monkey tribes, the ancestral apes did not resemble any of the primates that came before them. Bigger and heavier, they had deep chests, straighter backs, a more upright posture, and free-swinging arms.

In contrast with long-tailed monkeys, whose front and hind limbs were of almost equal length, apelike primates were tailless and had long arms and short legs. They differed from monkeys not only in size and structure but also in the way they moved about in the trees.

APELIKE PRIMATES COULD MOVE
THEIR ARMS FREELY IN ALL DIRECTIONS,
BENDING THEM AT THE ELBOW,
OR RAISING THEM OVER THEIR HEADS.

33

Instead of walking on the tops of branches, the apes traveled by swinging hand-over-hand from branch to branch. As a result, they developed extremely strong hands with elongated fingers which curved into hooks when hanging on branches. Their thumbs, by comparison, were very short and did not interfere with the hooking action of the fingers.

On the ground they usually walked on all fours, but for short distances they could travel on two legs. Their upright gait was waddling and awkward, because their hind legs were not built to support the entire body's weight. And their feet, which were really hands, were better for grasping than for walking.

While most of the early apelike primates were continuing their evolution in the treetops, one particular branch of the family had taken a separate path. We don't know exactly when or why, but this group of primates came down from the trees and learned to live on the ground.

This new way of life brought about some startling changes in the physical structure of these unusual primates. We can only surmise how it happened. One guess is that in exploring the plains away from the shelter of the trees they came to depend on their rotating arms and grasping hands for gathering food, capturing and subduing game, and defending themselves against enemies. With the hands occupied, the job of moving from place to place fell more and more on the hind limbs alone. In time the feet lost their handlike appearance and became better suited for walking.

These creatures had shorter arms than their forebears. They also stood erect on longer, better constructed legs. And their hands, when totally relieved of the burden of locomotion, were free to pursue a whole new set of activites.

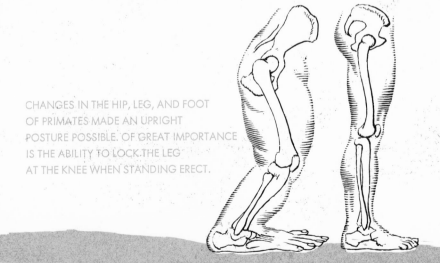

CHANGES IN THE HIP, LEG, AND FOOT
OF PRIMATES MADE AN UPRIGHT
POSTURE POSSIBLE. OF GREAT IMPORTANCE
IS THE ABILITY TO LOCK THE LEG
AT THE KNEE WHEN STANDING ERECT.

By the time the two-legged man-apes came into being, the hand was entering its final stage of development. Throughout the more than 300 million years of vertebrate evolution, its basic structure had been remodeled, improved, and passed on. First, it was a paddle for dragging the body over the ground. Then, it became a multitoed support for walking and running on the land. Later, it became a five-toed clamp for climbing trees, and still later, a grasping, hooklike hand for hanging and swinging from branches.

In its human arrangement, the five-fingered appendage was molded into a hand well-proportioned for manipulation. The thumb grew longer and achieved true opposability — it could come around and touch each of the other four fingers. And because it was no longer used for locomotion, the hand lost its calloused roughness and acquired an extremely delicate sense of touch.

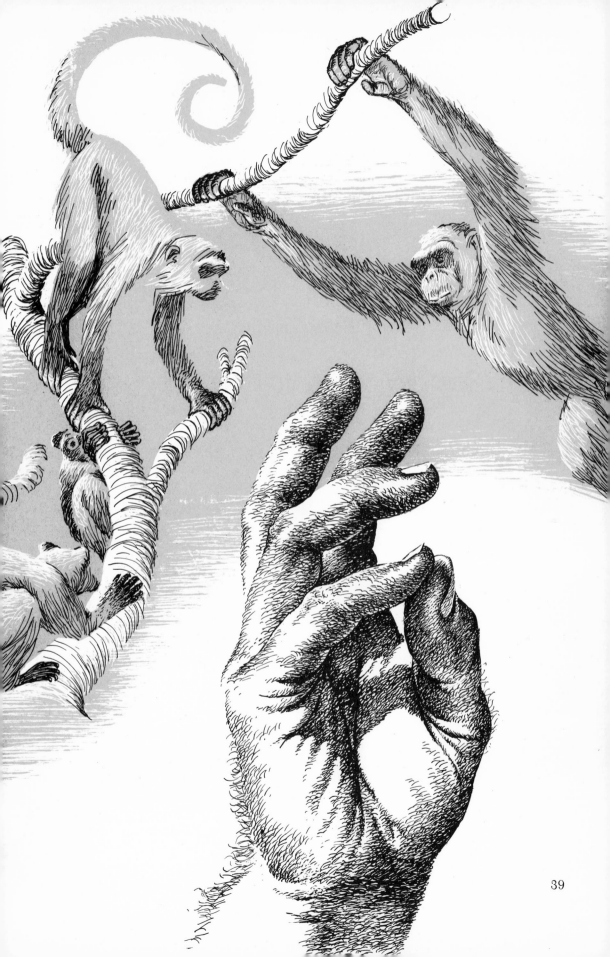

Just as erect posture brought about changes in apelike primates, such as the shortening of the arms and the reshaping of the spine, so the freeing of the hand changed apelike creatures into man-apes.

They used their hands for grasping and holding, for digging and tearing, for turning, twisting, and pushing. They came to depend on their hands to bring things close to their eyes, ears, nose, and mouth, to throw sticks and stones, to wield clubs. By touching an object with their fingers, they could learn if the surface was smooth or rough, if it was hard or soft, hot or cold.

All these diverse activities of the hand had to be co-ordinated in the brain. As the use of the hand increased, the motor and sensory parts of the brain grew larger. And with a larger brain came greater intelligence. Voluntary action increasingly replaced instinctive behavior, marking the appearance of a brand-new species — our species — *Homo sapiens*, Man the Wise.

Dextrous hands controlled by a thinking brain are the outstanding features which set early man apart from all other living things. From the time he first appeared on earth, man relied on a combination of skill and cunning to survive.

Early man lacked many of the natural weapons of his heavily armed neighbors. He had no fangs, no tusks, no claws, no horns, and no hoofs. His sight was not as sharp as that of predatory birds. Most of the lower animals had a keener sense of smell and hearing. Less intelligent creatures could outrun him, saber-toothed tigers could tear him apart, and mammoths could crush him.

Yet, the other inhabitants of man's hostile world were no match for him. He made efficient weapons to throw at his prey from a distance. He devised traps and snares to capture the huge or fleet-footed animals he needed for food.

Early man used his clever brain to outsmart his enemies. But his skillful hands made him the equal and, in time, the master of his fierce rivals.

Throughout his history, man has been a toolmaker. To be sure, his first tools were no more than the sharpened edges of stones. But he soon found ways to make hand axes for chopping trees, scrapers for shaping wood, cutters for skinning animals, and chisels for carving or splintering bones, antlers, and tusks into delicate articles such as fishhooks and needles.

With manipulative hands to serve his human brain, man learned to control his environment. He built shelters to keep himself safe and dry. He made clothes and kindled fires to keep himself warm. He discovered how to plant seeds, gather the harvest, and grind wheat into flour.

We can trace man's development from prehistoric times by the implements he made and discarded, by the ruins of the structures he put together, by the faded designs, decorations, paintings, and artifacts he created and left behind.

The human brain made man a civilized being — but it was his hands that recorded his progress and made human culture possible.

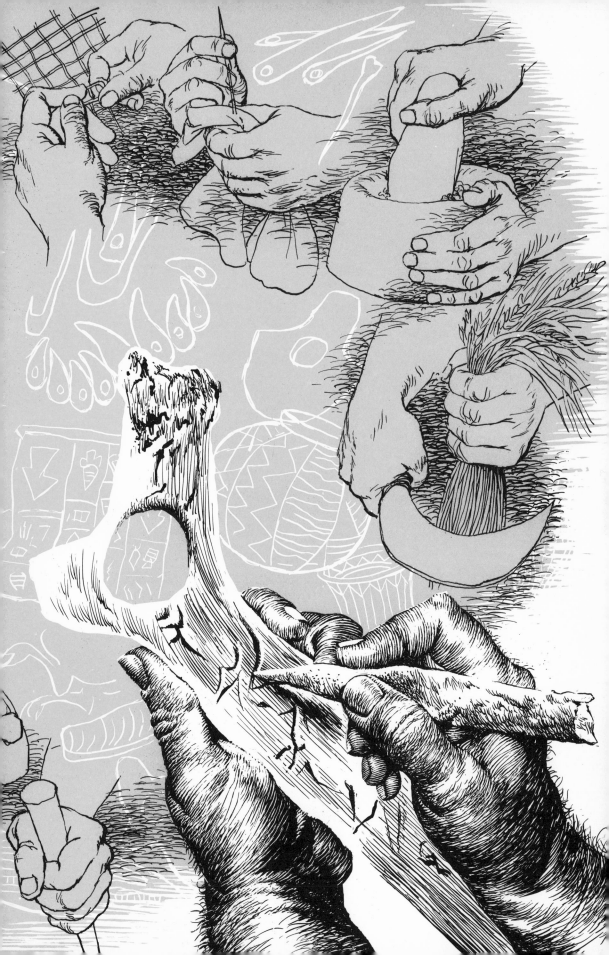

Today we live in an age of automation. Many of the tedious tasks which were once done by human hands are now performed by machines. Cranes, power shovels, and bulldozers do most of man's heavy work. Mechanical hands called manipulators are assigned his dangerous industrial chores.

But machines merely extend the capacities of the human hand. They can never duplicate the manual versatility of the human operator who controls these devices.

The work of artists, craftsmen, musicians, and surgeons testifies to the amazing ability of human hands to learn special skills. And the countless ways we use them in our routine, everyday lives are evidence of their dexterity.

Human hands are indeed one of man's most priceless possessions. It is impossible to imagine what our world would be like without them.